FOREWORD

Hello and thank you for purchasing approach to writing poetry is quite casual and instinctive. As a schoolteacher of nearly 30 years I know a little about structure and rhythm but I tend to just observe something while I'm out walking or driving and think "I'll write a poem about that tonight." And that is about it!

You will notice different rhyming patterns such as abcb, abab, aabb, etc as well as one or two limericks. I've tried to ensure the rhythm is usually kept constant but occasionally a sentence might be too long or too short to fit. My editing technique is quite relaxed so you may notice the odd grammar, spelling or punctuation error – hopefully not too many!

Most of the poems contain an opinion I held during a particular moment at a particular time on a particular date, but opinions change and evolve over time so please do not read anything dramatically profound into them. These poems are (generally) meant to be light – hearted although a few lean slightly towards melancholy. In these politically sensitive times I have tried to steer clear of offending anyone although large institutions such as politics, law and education are gently mocked, I'm sure they're used to it and are able to 'take it on the chin'.

Please feel free to e-mail feedback, good or bad, to me at philipjohnson2009@hotmail.com and if there's a sequel to this collection of literary nonsense I'll make sure I let you know? Thank you once more for spending a few hard-earned pennies or cents on this edition,

DEDICATED

To my two beautiful daughters, it has been an absolute honour being your Father.

May the privilege continue for a long, long time !

CONTENTS

1. IT'S GONE
2. TWITS ON TWITTER
3. 1975
4. AREN'T WE LUCKY ?
5. 6's AND 7's
6. CATS AN' DOGS ?
7. AS BIG AS A BRICK
8. BECKHAM
9. A DOG'S LIFE
10. POLITICIAN IN A STEW
11. HEROES
12. NEVER GIVE UP ON YER DREAMS
13. A SPECIAL NEED
14. 'EALTH AND SAFETY
15. APPRENTICE
16. WANT TO BE NUMBER 4
17. GRASS

18. GYM GUY

19. TRAFFIC WARDEN

20. TRAFFIC CONES

21. NEW CAR

22. BARTH AND LARF

23. RAINBOW OF HEADS

24. A.D.H.D.

25. FRENCH MOVIE

26. SOAPS

27. TOURISTS

28. FLY ON THE WALL

29. PUNCH ABOVE MY WEIGHT

30. NO BUSES

31. NEW TATTOO

32. OPENING NIGHT

33. WHAT'S YOUR NAME ?

34. EMPTY CHAIR

35. ORDINARY BLOKE

36. ABNORMAL LOAD

37. VISITOR TO SCHOOL

38. FISHIN'

39. FARMER

40. YER KIDZ

41. IN A RUSH

42. CINEMA

43. HAY FEVER

44. SCHOOL INSPECTOR

45. DOWN AND OUT

46. FOOTBALLER

47. POLICE

48. WEDDING D.J.

49. MUM'S GONE

50. STEP DADS

IMAGE CREDITS

Used with permission from Microsoft.

All images found by searching : http://office.microsoft.com/en-us/images

1. IT'S GONE

Men in pubs talking all night

Say what's wrong put the World right

Nothing too academic nothing too bright

Take a cigarette, ask for a light

Then there's the games : skittles, darts, pool

The equivalent of a Frenchman and his boule

Generally all good-natured, as a rule

Just average, normal, not too fashionable or cool

This has been the way for a century or four

All strands of society, rich, medium, poor

Rubbing shoulders, discussing the law

Politics, sport, content to casually bore

But it's going going gone as we speak

Beautiful architecture, heritage, once the peak

Of British culture, rowdy as well as meek

But it's dying, dozens shut down every week

What caused it ? This public house demise ?

Was it the tax on beer ? All the smoke was never wise

Was it cheap supermarket liquor, all those bargain buys ?

We all caused it to die – right in front of our eyes

2. TWITS ON TWITTER

What's going on ? Make a comment on Twitter

Who's hot who's not and at whom are we going to titter ?

Who's done their ironing and who's been shopping ?

Who's eating a box of chocs whilst channel – hopping ?

Who's sharing exclusive photos of their big night out ?

Who's missing a long lost cousin and giving them a shout ?

Who's promoting something really worthy ? Who's seen an incriminating snap of themselves and getting nervy ?

Who's gossiping and saying something mean ?

Who's wondering which diet is best and why they're no longer lean ?

Who's really pissed off with their neighbours and boyfriend Tom ?

Who's recommending their all time favourite rom – com ?

Who's not going to be seeing another man …… ever ?

And how many of us, when asked to join all this, say …… NEVER !

3.   1975

They say the 70's was the decade which lacked taste

The strikes, no electric, they wouldn't collect yer waste

I know the fashion was crap, but we all felt alive

And for that reason I wish it was still 1975

Flares were groovy, long hair was still cool

Platform shoes and kipper ties allowed at school

High waistband trousers well before Simon Cowell

Pychotic actors like Malcolm McDowell

Glam rock, wig wam bam, Philadelphia funk

Zany and off the wall, the anarchy of punk

Smoking on buses, in cinemas and in pubs

Infra-red flashing disco lights in clubs

Yes it was always raining, always grey and wet

And the most fun yer dad could have was a cheeky bet

But we thought it was great, everything new and weird

And like today, young men thought girls liked a beard

If they invented a working time machine

I'd go straight back and enjoy being seen

In boutiques, on football terraces and in bars

Then stepping out in one of Ford's cars

A Cortina perhaps or even a Capri

With a double for Donny's sister Marie

Into nostalgia is where we all sometimes dive

But sadly it'll never again be 1975

4. AREN'T WE LUCKY ?

I once read that the English are life's lottery winners

Not only do we have breakfast and lunch we also have dinners

No wonder we have obesity issues

But there are others for whom we should take out the tissues

Through none of our own skill and purely luck

Out of this globe our forefathers made a handsome buck

Helping our towns and economy to flourish

So all our post-Victorian children are happily nourished

Not the same can be said for the rest of the World

For some, war and poverty is all that's unfurled

Are we grateful, really ? Do we appreciate it ?

Are we humble and modest when applying our wit ?

Or do we scorn and grumble and point faults in our lot ?

Whilst denying that what we have was immorally got

The diversity in our existence offers choices

Whilst others just survive and do not have voices

Their killing fields and horrors are real

Whilst we dispute the discount on a meal deal

So when our father's fish swam into our mother's womb

Thank your stars it was in a nation that once enjoyed boom

Another place at another time in another time zone

And your fate would truly justify your groan

5.   6's AND 7's

"I'm all at sixes and sevens" : what a strange phrase

Does anyone even use that statement these days ?

What does "at sixes and sevens" actually mean ?

Why not the number eleven or even seventeen ?

What have they got against fours and fives ?

For those two numbers they've got out the knives !

And what's so wrong with eights and nines ?

Through those two numbers they've drawn thick red lines

"ooh I'm all muddled up I'm at sixes and sevens"

Sounds almost as old-fashioned as saying "Good Heavens"

Why don't we all rebel against this norm, who agrees ?

Next time you're mixed up say "I'm all at two's and three's"

And when we're feeling anarchic and a little bit mean

We'll say "I feel funny, I'm at twelves and thirteen"

6.   CATS AN' DOGS ?

Where does 'raining cats and dogs' come from ?

Have you ever had to dodge falling alsatians or even a Tom ?

It doesn't make sense it's got me puzzled

I've never seen flying dogs whether or not they're muzzled

It's only raindrops you need to check the sky for

You're hardly likely to see a tail, whisker or paw ?

You might see ominous dark clouds which fill you with dread

But you won't get a Doberman dropping on your head

When we feel the sun's rays we tend to be merrier

That's way more likely than a shower of Yorkshire terrier

In a newspaper, the weather forecast you've found

Will never include a reference to corgi or daschaund

It's rain from the heavens which feeds your flowers

Not a cacophony of descending tabbies or chihauhas

So next time anyone says it's 'raining cats and dogs'

Tell them there's more chance of it 'snowing bats and frogs' !

7. AS BIG AS A BRICK

I want a mobile telephone as big as a brick

Even though some would point and shout "look at that dick !"

Yes it would stand out, yes it would look naff

But it would bring smiles to faces, a joke, a laugh

The ringtone on it would be dated and sad

The size of it alone would suggest I'm quite mad

I'd shout really loud, like Dom Jolly, HELL – OH !!

And enjoy the authority it would give me to bellow

So you can sling your slimline smug phone that's a centimetre thick

I don't care 'cause I want one as big as a brick

8. BECKHAM

Does he ever do anything outrageously normal, that David Beckham ?

Like buy a kilo of tomatoes on the high street in Peckham ?

Or stand at the bar being boring in his local ?

Or shout at the telly being far too vocal ?

Does he visit gran and hear about 'the good old days' ?

Or check his lottery ticket at the shop to see if it pays ?

Does he call a mobile phone store to query his bill ?

Or check his nectar point card and see the balance is nil ?

Does he forget to put the sugar in his cup of tea ?

Or look for bargains 'buy one get one free' ?

Does he argue with a rival dad on the school yard and threaten to deck 'em ?

Well obviously not, afterall, he's David Beckham !

9. A DOG'S LIFE

It's a dog's life, so they say

On this blanket I merrily lay

And wait for owner to pat me on the head

Then after breakfast I'll be led

To my favourite field, playground or park

To see some four-legged friends at whom I'll bark

We'll bound along, run, race and sniff

Maybe searching for a familiar whiff

Then home for more adulation and praise

Has owner got 'owt else to do with his days ?

Another bowl of biscuits and meat

I wonder if 'children in need' have such a treat ?

I'm loving it, warm house, carpet, warm bed

No longer for us outdoor kennels or shed

We've moved indoors now, family member, one of the team

We ain't going back outside, only in a nightmare-ish dream

That nonsense is for rabbits or a cat

We're all cosy, lounging by the fire, so take that !

10. POLITICIAN IN A STEW

I guess I'm just another politician in a stew

One constituent ran up to me, shouted "Oi you !

With yer fake morality, fake ethics, fake grin

You don't care about us while sipping yer gin !

A Labour M.P. was always a trade union member

Would put on a party for miners' kids in December

Would walk around terraced houses knocking on doors

Would need to check his pools coupon for any score draws

Would like a pint, maybe smoke a pipe

Would eat fish and chips, sometimes trotters or tripe

But all that changed with New Labour, Brown and Blair

You're no longer from round here, you're from .....well......over there !

With yer barrister's background and yer Oxbridge past

You can retire to the country on the wealth you've amassed"

"OK....alright....you've had your say

Oh here's my chauffeur to collect me......good day !"

11. HEROES

Who are your heroes ? Do you believe in them ?

Would you trust them with your life ?

Can they fight off villains, monsters, bad guys ?

Are they good with their fists, a gun, a knife ?

What do you want from them, the ability to protect ?

Must they wear a cape or a coat of steel ?

Do they have to wear thick strong underpants ?

Do they have to be imaginary or real ?

Do they have to be from another galaxy or will Earth do ?

Do you place high expectations on your personal hero ?

As long as he or she can answer the phone, mow the lawn

Is that enough ? Is the pressure on them virtually zero ?

In my eyes someone who helps an O.A.P. cross the road

Or checks on a neighbour or says hello to a stranger

Has done enough to be classed as a hero

If the World was full of them, no-one would be in danger

12. NEVER GIVE UP ON YER DREAMS

Don't give up on your dreams kids   Keep those hopes alive

I wanted to be a superhero   From the age of about
five

Don't give up on your dreams kids   Think of new ones, it's
never too late

I wanted to play football for England   From the age of eight

Don't give up on your dreams kids   There'll be chances again
and again

I wanted to be an astronaut with Neil Armstrong   From the age of
ten

Don't give up on your dreams kids   Things to experience and
new tricks

I became a school teacher   At the age of twenty six

It seems so long ago now   When I first saw kids'
smiling faces

Ran football teams basketball teams   Organised athletics races

Think of all those who came to the school and went   Where did
the years go ?

What happened to them all ?   There's so many I
couldn't possibly know

Each making their own path in life   Each starting an individual
story

Some of them will have a quiet time   Others will want success
and glory

Everyone's unique everyone's special   We've all got something we can do

Use your skills as best as you can   Don't do it for others - do it for you !

Please don't give up on your dreams kids   You don't need to ask why

Be good for your teachers and parents   Just keep those hopes sky-high !

13. A SPECIAL NEED

These days there's loads with a special need

But not for me, I don't get it

Sometimes it gets on my nerves

But mostly, I try not to let it

Someone's got a lisp someone's got a stammer

And a few people have a phobia of bees

Someone hates bananas another hates grapes

They claim something in 'em makes 'em sneeze

Someone has a fear of flying

Others are allergic to flowers

Someone gets anxious in crowded places

Some people's skin is no good in showers

At times I wish I had a special need

And have my condition assessed – all formal

But I ain't got any symptoms and so

I'll have to assume I'm 'normal' ?

14. 'EALTH AND SAFETY

Put those scissors down you'll hurt yourself

Make sure you don't knock anything off the shelf

Cover those ear-rings you might scratch yourself

Put those biscuits down, you'll suffer ill-health

Don't do headstands you might have a headache

Don't do backward rolls you might have a backache

Don't do cartwheels for your arms' sake

Don't do handstands your hands might break

The floor's slippy you need grip on your shoes

And check fire exits you've seen what happens on the news

No plastic bits to swallow allowed, nor tins, nor glass

All appliances must be checked daily for escaping gas

No food allowed past 'sell by date' in case it's rotten

Which year did we start wrapping children in cotton ?

Surely the 'ealth and safety brigade have got it wrong ?

'Cause all us adults today managed to live this long

15. APPRENTICE

Have you seen those contestants on The Apprentice ?

Running around for the fame and the glory ?

One minute selling the next producing

All talking a far-fetched story

They all seem to think it's good

To say they'd gladly tread on others

And treat their fellow contestants

In ways intolerable to their mothers

They all want to reach the final episode

And partner Donald (U.S.) or Alan (U.K.)

They all seem to think they're talented

And should be project manager with the biggest say

But they dither and dilly dally and

Rarely live up to the task

"Just how deluded am I ?"

Is the only question they need to ask

16. WANT TO BE NUMBER 4

I realise I'm only number 16

On your closest person's list

I ache when I don't see you

For you I guess I'm rarely missed

Your life is full of things going on

Happenings, and things 'going down'

I can only contact you so much

To over-do it might make you frown

I wish I were more significant

I wish I were in your World

I wish a lot more often

My arms around you could be curled

I'll accept it and won't go on

And turn into a bore

But when I'm drunk I fantasize

I'm not number 16 but really number 4 !

17. GRASS

There it is .... the incessant drone of the lawn mower

The badge of the middle class gardening grass – grower

Surely there's something more fun he could do

Than walking up and down up and down phew !

What repetition, groundhog day indeed

To try and eliminate the dreaded weed

It's a battle that ultimately has no winner

At breakfast the lawn might be ahead but not by dinner

Because an array of weapons, spades and trowel

Will work until nature throws in the towel

OK OK you're ahead, we're a domestic garden

If we become wild your resolve will harden

Then you'll dig and chop and trim and cut

To get us into shape and look tidy ......but

The moment you go away for a week's break

We'll grow and grow, our young roots awake

We'll be back in business, standing real tall

When you return you'll see we haven't behaved at all

It's pointless calling for the demise of the horticultural community

I'm afraid they'll be busy for an absolute eternity

18. GYM GUY

Man at the gym, man at the gym

Running like mad, would you just look at him ?

He's sweating a pool, sweating like rain

Blood vessels bursting, no pain no gain

Pushing iron pumping iron three hours a day

Gotta keep those abs tight, you know what they'll say ?

Wants to mimic Arnie when he was in his prime

Wants to look huuuuge – is that such a crime ?

Burning calories, building muscle

Rivals psyched out, he knows how to hustle

Press-ups, sit-ups, crunches, dips

Can't afford days off, can't afford blips

Who can keep up with man at the gym ?

Why'd you want to punish every single limb ?

19. TRAFFIC WARDEN

There's a traffic warden issuing each ticket

At the speed a fast bowler knocks down a wicket

He's an eager beaver, he's super keen

In the last half hour he's dished out fifteen

There's no stopping him, he's not giving up now

He's on fire and he's sweating from his brow

He doesn't give a damn what the public think

And he's not afraid to 'cause a stink'

Amongst a community trying to park in town

But this 'bastion of the law' wants to 'take 'em down'

He doesn't care if they're rushing to the bank

For a nice juicy fine they have him to thank

He doesn't care if they're at the pharmacy

With their prescription to fight off pleurisy

If they overstay their parking time by half a min

They're going straight into traffic warden's 'sin bin'

20. TRAFFIC CONES

Traffic cones, lots and lots of 'em

Set out on a Monday morning

For the remainder of the week

In huge queues we'll all be yawning

Some workmen do some work

And some new features are made

You'd expect that wouldn't you ?

Afterall, that's why they're paid

So job partly completed, almost done

The end of the week virtually here

You're thinking : cones will be gone

All lanes open : let's cheer !

But you're wrong, it ain't that simple

Too much trouble to collect

We'll leave the cones where they are

Despite drivers' weekends being wrecked

So Saturday and Sunday we use that route

Cones standing proudly upright and tall

But there's no workmen working, they're all at home

So all we can do is ....cr...a....w......l ......

21. NEW CAR

I've got a new car, it's red, glossy and sleek

Been saving up for ages, I got it last week

The wheels are silver, the steering wheel's leather

It makes me a winner, no matter what the weather

'Cause it's got a soft top you can raise in the sun

Makes it seem like the lottery I've just gone and won

If it's not rush hour and the highway's clear

I like to slip the gearstick into fifth gear

The road-users envy me as I glide past

They've probably not seen a car hurtle this fast ?

But was that a flash ? Did something go 'zap' ?

Oh no, the speed camera's taken a snap

There'll be a penalty, an officer might call

Perhaps I'm not so impressive after all ?

22. BARTH AND LARF

You know how us in the North say, with a short 'a' ....bath

And how it kind of makes those Southerners ....laugh

'Cause they think they've got it right by saying "I'll take a barth"

Or on recounting the night before will say "It was such a larf"

Well I hate to disappoint them but I have some bad news

Despite our dialect, for many years, having caused them amuse

In fact our diction is phonetically correct

I'd go as far as saying it's totally perfect

Because in words such as mast, last and past

There's no bloody letter R ....get over it, fast !

23. RAINBOW OF HEADS

There's a rainbow forming everywhere

And it's nowhere near the sky

It's emerging on heads of hair

And no-one's quite sure why

It tends to be ladies of a certain age

Though younger are afflicted too

Next thing pensioners will be in on the act

No longer, for their rinse, choosing only blue

Shocking red is quite popular

Purple can be seen in every town

Maybe people who crave attention

Use it as a deterrent to 'feeling down' ?

Not anymore just gothics and punks

We've now got solicitors and teachers who think

There's nowt wrong with having green hair

Or a 'bonce' that's all shocking pink

24. ADHD

Abusive kid in class, hurts someone with his knee

"Yeah but I can't help it mate, I've got ADHD"

Doesn't listen in class, shouts at Simon and Lee

"Don't know I'm doing it pal, it's the ADHD"

If there's such a deficit of attention

For someone who has this condition

Why is it that when there's an addition

To his PSP or DS games collection

He can bloody well concentrate all night

Without so much as a snack to bite

Seeing stuff that would normally fright

Yet we're supposed to believe he just might

Be afflicted with something really unfortunate

And, you know, it makes him kind of desperate

It might even explain why he's illiterate

And that no-one should have to suffer this fate

But while Jimmy spits and proceeds to curse

The rest of the class try to study verse

And for the other 29 there's nothing worse

No wonder poor teacher gets a little terse !

25. FRENCH MOVIE

Have you ever seen a French movie ?

'Film noir' I think is the name

There's lots of moody glances

Plus of course the occasional "Je t'aime"

When you next watch a French movie

Check out how the actors look cool

The leading lady is always sensual

And the leading man makes her drool

They smoke gitanes cigarettes in Paris

And speak philosophically about life

Then they retire to a hotel room

At seven he returns to his wife

The woman is full of self-loathing

And threatens to 'end it all' with passion

He whisperingly talks her out of it

Then buys her a dress that's in fashion

Once more she feels like Sophia Loren

Sips coffee at a cafe on the Left Bank

But monsieur fails to contact her

So her heart, once again, has sank

Have you tried to follow a French movie

With no subtitles ? It's tough

The actors are arrogant and suave

They make us feel we're not good enough !

26. SOAPS

Some of us love soaps, not really myself

I don't have box sets of DVD's on every shelf

Apparently it's art imitating life

The tension you can cut it with a knife

But the writers are generally from safe backgrounds

They won't have been in pubs buying rounds

Not sure what gives them the sort of right

Onto which ordinary lives they can shine a light ?

Doubt if they've ever gone hungry or had a scrap

Doubt if they've been skint or had a major mishap

Doubt if they've lived in a working class zone

Doubt if they've had to face a threatening tone

So what makes 'em think that in every street

There's a rapist, a killer, thieves every few feet ?

Exaggerated drivel that makes 'em feel good

That they live in a classier neighbourhood

Sometimes they catch a community's life accurately

But they also condescend and patronise woefully

27. TOURISTS

We're herded around like cattle

We're tourists living the dream

We've been to Caesar's Palace, Champs Elysee

We've paid ten euro's for ice cream

Yes we're naive and innocent

Yes we probably trust too much

Place us in the centre of Amsterdam

We'll talk English AND double-Dutch

The gondoliers of Venice

Spot us from a mile away

"Ciao, bongiorno, bella mia"

But for this charm we'll have to pay

We're quite harmless usually

We help keep economies afloat

We're always looking for some escape

By train, aeroplane or boat

We don't mind a bit of culture

Paella or sangria in Spain

Lasagne and pasta in Italy

As long as there's chips with the main

28. FLY ON THE WALL

If only I could be a fly on the wall

I'd see what first year students got up to at the fresher's ball

Straight back to halls banging each other

No cares about how's yer father or who's yer mother

Away from home for the first time in life

No-one to instruct or guide like a parent or wife

Anything possible, potentially everyone for anyone

Alcohol, fags and drugs an alternative medicine

Reckless, mad, debauched, carefree

They wonder how did they contract that S.T.D. ?

29. PUNCH ABOVE MY WEIGHT

Gonna punch above my weight and ask out Nicole Scherzinger

Do me a favour mate, we've only ever seen you with a minger

If that fails I'll go for Britney Spears

Didn't you hear what happened in Vegas ? It'll end in tears

Yeah OK well I could ask Angelina Jolie

But you've not saved the World, you're not righteous or holy

Your eyes will be popping when you see me out with Kelly Brook

Mate she'll definitely turn you down without even one look

I could get down and funky and go for Beyonce

Well Jay Zee's her husband so you won't make it to fiancé

I suppose there's always Cameron Diaz

But she'd normally go for someone with more pizz-azz

There's always the glamorous Penelope Cruz

But she'd want someone actually in the news

I could be really adventurous and try contacting Princess Kate

You've no blue blood in yer veins and you're a couple of years late

I could claim to be musical and try for Rihanna

You can't sing, you can't dance, you've never touched a piano

Who's down on her luck and maybe not so fussy ? Demi Moore

Just get real and go ask out her with no teeth from next door !

30. NO BUSES

['Chell Heath' could be substituted with the name of any urban district which has relatively low income or high unemployment. The poem doesn't criticise Chell Heath, it criticises people's attitudes towards an estate which might have something of a reputation.]

You know Chell Heath, do any buses go there ?

No I've asked the drivers and none of 'em would dare

Come on, it's Chell Heath, there must be some buses that go there ?

I've asked time and again, they're not brave, they're too square

But Chell Heath, why can't any buses go there ?

I met the drivers' union rep, he just gave me this stare

It's only Chell Heath, not the Bronx, why not drive there ?

The drivers' health and safety, we do have to take care

But apart from Chell Heath you lot'll drive anywhere

I know son, accept it, some things in life just ain't fair !

31. NEW TATTOO

I've got a brand new tattoo

That makes me harder than you

I ain't got a single tattoo

That makes me more secure than you

I've got a brand new tattoo

That makes me edgier than you

I ain't got a single tattoo

That makes me more confident than you

I've got a brand new tattoo

That makes me slicker than you

I ain't got a single tattoo

That makes me smarter than you

I've got a brand new tattoo

That makes me cooler than you

I ain't got a single tattoo

That makes me more rounded than you !

32. OPENING NIGHT

We're at the theatre it's the opening night

Nerves and not an empty seat in sight

The usher's been ushering, the programmes all sold

But I'm the leading man and I've got a cold

Tried 'em all, tablets, hot lemon, tissues

None of it's worked, help, I've got issues

On the audience front row I'll be spluttering

If I'm about to sneeze, my lines I'll be stuttering

My voice is a foghorn 'cause my nose is bunged up

Hey stagehand, do us some water in a cup ?

Bluff my way through this, I'll have to for sure

If only someone had come up with a dead-cert cure

I wouldn't have to be dealing with this stress

And my handkerchief wouldn't contain this 'orrible mess

33. WHAT'S YOUR NAME ?

Hiya, where you from ? What's your name ?

Speak to strangers ? That's not my game

Hey, where you from ? what's your name ?

I won't be telling you, what a shame !

Oi ! Where you from ? What's your name ?

Is that all you can say ? Pretty lame !

D'ya hear, where you from ? What's your name ?

I'm more into macho men, you're too tame

I SAID... where you from ? What's your name ?

Not really into low-life, I'm after fame

For the last time, where you from ? What's your name ?

That your best chat-up line ? You men are all the same !

34. EMPTY CHAIR

There's a great big empty chair

Our kid used to sit in it, over there

Out of the window he would happily stare

But he's gone now, you might ask where

It was his turn in life's lottery to go

A fair bit too soon, I know

All those chances in life you blow

He was no different and so ……….

Live life to the full if you can

Don't let the years slip idly 'down the pan'

Be a bit daring, you don't have to be Action Man

Smile, give frowning a permanent ban

35. ORDINARY BLOKE

When you're an ordinary bloke

Who happens to come from Stoke

They think we're all thick, not sharp or quick

And assume yer I.Q. is a joke

When you're an ordinary bloke

Who happens to come from Stoke

They seem overjoyed, half of us unemployed

And they know that we're all fairly broke

When you're an ordinary bloke

Who happens to come from Stoke

They think it's ironic and smile, that we miss Jeremy Kyle

'Cause at mid-day we still haven't woke

When you're an ordinary bloke

Who happens to come from Stoke

They say we're not fit, we don't care one bit

And we're always after a smoke

When you're an ordinary bloke

Who happens to come from Stoke

They say that in drugs we deal, as if that's actually real ?

We're not ALL into smack, crack and coke !

36. ABNORMAL LOAD

Have you ever noticed a sign by the road

Warning you of an abnormal load ?

Now that's helpful and useful for us drivers

But there's something that bothers me, it mothers

Just what is a load that is normal ?

Is there a guideline, has it been made formal ?

If someone has nothing in their car, is that subnormal ?

Perhaps a ghost on board is classed as paranormal ?

Maybe five hefty people is too heavy a load

If only one handbag then that's a bit light for the road

We're never warned about an underweight lorry

It's a code unfairly biased towards bulk – sorry !

37. VISITOR TO SCHOOL

Teachers get really tetchy and stressed

When there's a visitor who's supposed to be impressed

With their school and each 'perfect' child

Suppressed kids who've been told for today to "act mild"

Staff hope they'll shut up and listen

And each one will display smiles that glisten

But the reality is they could turn ratty

If the visitor's talk starts to drive 'em batty

Youngsters usually cope for quarter of an hour

But then they could suss out that the visitor's quite dour

"His talk's not stimulating – in fact it's pants –

Like watching paint dry or the snail-slow growth of plants"

Then they slaughter him with fidgeting and abuse

He pleads with the Head, "They won – let me loose !"

38. FISHIN'

Fishing on the riverbank fishing in the sea

Fishing on a lake ....Is it just me ?

Who can argue the point of this aimless life ?

Or is it just a convenient escape from the wife ?

And not just for an hour or two – sometimes all night

Returning home with grubby hands and smelly wellies at daylight

I don't get it, it's not for me, perhaps I'm too wild

Maybe to qualify to fish you should be meditative and mild ?

39. FARMER

A farmer's life, rural, serene

On venturing into town they're not too keen

All those noisy people, all that bustle

They'd rather hear leaves in the wind gently rustle

Banks, shops, car parks, trains

They'd rather amble slowly along country lanes

Offices, bus stops, police stations, graffiti

They'd rather see a field of corn or one that's all wheaty

Rude people shouting, aggression, bad manners

They'd rather mend a rusty old tractor with spanners

Concrete, tarmac, steel, blocks of flats

They'd rather a simple "good morning" while tilting their hats

40. YER KIDZ

Do yer kids.......realise you care ?

Do they notice you, do they realise you're there ?

Do they value that – to see them – you'd walk anywhere ?

Do they value that all of your's, with them, you'd gladly share ?

Do yer kids .... appreciate your protective cotton glove ?

Or that, compared to anyone else, you place 'em above ?

Do they know that, if you could, you'd send a dove

To bring peace to them when they've fallen out of love ?

You'd give your kidney, your lungs, your heart, your brain

If it meant prolonging their life ? That priority would be main

Do they know your love is unstoppable, like a runaway train ?

It's unconditional, is given always, and will never wane

41. IN A RUSH

I'm in a rush I'm in a hurry

Dodging around cars I scurry

Swapping lanes swapping gears

Been driving like this for many years

Always to the speed limit I'm very close

Those well under it must be boring, morose

I don't understand taking your time

For me, anything less than frantic is a crime

Who's this in front ? oi, granddad get out the way

Stick to country lanes and only on Sunday

I'm revving, accelerating, overtaking

If you're left in my trail it's of your own making

Gonna rip past this Polo in lane two

Ha ha ! See him frown ? "yeah, same to you"

When I'm in the pub on my first drink

He'll be sitting in rush hour with time to think

About forgotten dreams, a forgotten life

Only to return to a home full of strife

It's a few minutes now since I went past him

He looked so slow, so pedestrian and dim

But I forgot that this route out of town

Has roundabouts and sets of lights to slow you down

Now it's me crawling in lane two....damn

And who's that coming past ? no, it's Polo man

42. CINEMA

Why do people use the cinema

What's their motive for attending the flicks ?

I've been a fanatic for many years

Since about the age of six

Why do people use the cinema

What's their motive for attending the flicks ?

Many of us go regularly

We need a weekly, or monthly, fix

Why do people use the cinema

What's their motive for attending the flicks ?

Well there's romance, drama, suspense, action

So much variety, take your picks

Why do people use the cinema

What's their motive for attending the flicks ?

Some go there to play on their phones

Have conversations, all sorts of tricks

Why do people use the cinema

What's their motive for attending the flicks ?

Making unnecessary noise

Don't you know you all get on our 'wicks' ?

43. HAY FEVER

If there is an actual creator

Why did he give us hay fever ?

Raw red eyes and dripping nose

I don't really like either

It messes up your routines

And if your girlfriend has hay fever

I guarantee that by the end of May

You'll seriously want to leave her

It makes you ratty, tired and angry

When it kicks in – that hay fever

You'll be on a very short fuse

You'll become the world's biggest diva

That pollen's a right bummer

It's the crap that gives us hay fever

Before it arrives we're polite and balanced

But once it hits - we're neither !

44. SCHOOL INSPECTOR

Schools Inspectors (from 'Ofsted') ....knobs

Big ego's big actors big gobs

They were mediocre teachers, some were flops

But their arrogance suggests they were 'tops' ?

Their schools were glad they broke rank

And joined the illustrious pseudo think-tank

Of educators who need to critique

Though their own performance was often weak

They couldn't cope in front of a tricky class

But on teachers' hearts and souls they trespass

Trampling on their dreams and ambition

While negativity is the only condition

They bring to a wide range of schools

Talking down to staff as if they're fools

And praising the least co-operative child

Whilst spouting excuses why they're so wild

They've forgotten lots and learnt zero

To survive in some schools today is to be a hero

Bad behaviour, exam stress, red tape, paperwork

Takes up your whole life, we're not able to shirk

So Inspectors, smell the coffee, get real

You used to be our colleagues so, while scoffing that expense-paid meal

Think back to when you had to teach, manage, assess and plan

And try to re-gain some empathy for your fellow woman and man

45. DOWN AND OUT

When you're down and feeling low

And find it impossible to glow

You can't be bothered to say hello

And if people ask you out it's, "no !"

You're probably slightly depressed

Your morale will be facing a test

Other people by now will have guessed

You're low in spirit, you're not at your best

Your whole persona is shaded blue

You'd cheer up if only you had a clue

How to shake it off, how to just pull through

But you're not alone, this condition's not new

It's true that your future's laden with doom

And on any topic you only see gloom

You've lost your mojo, your 'va va voom'

Now can everyone just get outta the room ?

46. FOOTBALLER

Preened footballers, acting cool

Of their fans they don't give a toss

They're only loyal to their accountant

Their agent and sometimes their Boss

It's quite important they stay in the team

So they'll listen to his pre-match talk

But as soon as a better offer comes their way

They tear up their contract and walk

It's ridiculous how they earn in a week

What most of us earn in a year

Do they care for the club ? 'cause when things get tough

They hastily seek a transfer

Their wives and girlfriends stay close

As their maintenance levels are high

'Miss' will panic when other 'hot babes' surround

She can spot the gold diggers nearby

With endorsements and sponsorship deals

When is there time to kick a ball ?

One phrase they should all bear in mind is

'Pride comes before a fall' !

47. POLICE

Police work today, an impossible task

But they do sometimes hide behind that public mask

Of officialdom, jobsworth and 'these is the rules'

Treating us like we're serial crooks or drug mules

Generally innocent, law abiding, hard-working souls

Might have mis-demeanoured while achieving their goals

Of attending a meeting or delivering a phone

But have driven 35 in a 30 m.p.h. zone

Now a cop with discretion or common sense

Might suggest to the driver he'll need to re-compense

Officers of the court if he does it once more

Sadly, police tend not to apply such reasoning before law

And so our banker, salesman, teacher or driver

Has to be placed through un-necessary mither

Of three points on his licence and a hefty fine

Which could have paid, for two, fine dining with wine

Meanwhile addicts, junkies, violent thugs

Seem immune, at times, with casual shrugs

To the same restrictions on their civil lifestyle

As they continue offending with a wink and wry smile

48. WEDDING D.J.

Why do wedding D.J.'s sometimes get it wrong

A few play wrong-choice music all night long

Gran hits the dance floor 'cause she's had her nap

So cool D.J. starts to play gangsta rap

Some teenagers hit the dance floor, looking bright

D.J. puts on Elvis, 'Are You Lonesome Tonight ?'

He just doesn't get it, does he, not a clue

That all age groups are <u>not</u> into The Who

Now your Uncle Ted and his wife Aunt Polly

Might enjoy Bill Hayley and Buddy Holly

But not everyone will appreciate it, obviously

In the same way O.A.P.'s don't dig Jay Zee

So clue-up Mr D.J. and keep an eye on the dance floor

Check out when it's buzzing and don't be a bore

By spoiling things with a sudden change in style

If it's jumpin' just leave-it-be for a while

49. MUM'S GONE

No-one can prepare you for it

When your Mother dies

They'll tell you that time heals

They'll tell you all sorts of lies

Nothing can make it better

Nothing takes away the pain

Nothing makes sense anymore

Nothing will be the same again

My Gran hit the nail on the head

The mother is the core

Of the whole family

Without her everything's raw

Nothing feels warm

Nothing feels gentle

Everything's cold and stark

Everyone's gone mental

Years later, there's still a gap in your heart

And you're not quite the same man

But I'm trying, at last, to move on

Just for you Mum, I'll see if I can

50. STEP DADS

Step dads are crap aren't they ?

'Cause no matter what they do and what they say

They'll never replace biological Dad

And they'll always come out looking a bit sad

They try to be funny, no-one smiles

This might be after driving step-kids around for miles

To the homes of friends who won't be Step Dad's friends

No matter how many shelves or bicycles he mends

He's onto a loser and he knows full – well

He'll never be liked despite the hard sell

It'll be the same in any step-home

May as well talk to the step dog or step garden gnome

'Cause no-one's bothered about him, no-one cares

And if he so much as dares

To point this out, he'll look a bit daft

Someone rescue him, send an emotional life-raft !

Printed in Great Britain
by Amazon.co.uk, Ltd.,
Marston Gate.